ILLUSTRATED BY EDWARD KOREN

Don't Talk to Strange Bears

The People Maybe

Cooking for Crowds

Noodles Galore

How to Eat Like a Child

Dragons Hate to Be Discreet

Teenage Romance

Do I Have to Say Hello?

A Dog's Life

ALSO BY EDWARD KOREN

Behind the Wheel

Do You Want to Talk About It?

Are You Happy?

Well, There's Your Problem

Caution, Small Ensembles

What About Me?

QUALITY TIME

VILLARD BOOKS • NEW YORK • 1995

QUALITY TIME

PARENTING, PROGENY, AND PETS

EDWARD KOREN

All rights reserved under International and Pan-American Copyright Conventions.
Published in the United States by Villard Books, a division of Random House, Inc.,
New York, and simultaneously in Canada by Random House of Canada Limited, Toronto.

Villard Books is a registered trademark of Random House, Inc.

Of the 124 drawings in this collection, 118 appeared
originally in *The New Yorker* and were copyrighted © in
the years 1969, 1974, and 1976 through 1995 inclusive by
The New Yorker Magazine, Inc.

Library of Congress Cataloging-in-Publication Data

Koren, Edward,
Quality time: parenting, progeny, and pets / by Edward Koren.
p.   cm.
ISBN 0-679-44436-X
1. Family—Caricatures and cartoons.   2. American wit and humor,
Pictorial.   I. Title.
NC1429.K62A4   1995
741.5'973–dc20   95-7767

Manufactured in the United States of America on acid-free paper
9 8 7 6 5 4 3 2
First Edition
Book design by Jo Anne Metsch

To the enduring memory and inspiration of
Daniel Robbins

Introduction

I have always been willing, unselfishly, to interrupt my own very important work to offer Edward Koren advice and ideas. In the small village in northern Vermont where Ed spends most of his time, he is a struggling volunteer fireman. He also has an office at *The New Yorker*. Often, as Ed passed my door on his way to the art department to submit rough sketches or finished drawings, I would invite him in—to lend encouragement or to reassure him that there is still value and meaning in a life with too few fires. Scrutinizing his work, I would offer specific suggestions that, I felt, would enhance his artistic endeavors.

Too vividly, I recall the time I told Ed that the characters in several of his drawings looked rather shaggy: Perhaps he should consider giving them more refined, sleek contours? Ed immediately became sullen. His characters have remained quite shaggy, defiantly so.

On another occasion I dared to let Ed know that his noses struck me as disproportionately large. I said this in a jocular tone: "Oh, Ed, so I see you've decided to include human figures as appendages to those noses you've been drawing." Ed is a mutterer, but as he left the room I clearly heard him refer to me as "an astounding cretin." In the months that followed, I discovered my own name featured in several drawings in which characters with larger-than-ever noses were placed in ludicrous situations.

Ed tends to depict adults, especially adult males, as preening dunces;

his women, in their silly attempts to be perfect mommies, also grate. Children, on the other hand, come off as precociously sharp-witted, even when they are being insolent. Ed's anthropomorphic renderings of clever animals, plants, and inanimate objects—always so playfully droll, never oafish or dull—raise interesting questions. I leave it to Ed's target audience: Are grownups, typically, self-deluded cant-spouting hypocrites? Were children and the other species put on this planet to make the rest of us look foolish? In principle, I am all for frivolity, in proper measures, but I wonder if Ed is playing fair. Does Ed Koren, perhaps, indulge in irresponsible whimsicality?

Ed's drawings are so generously detailed one must wonder whether he isn't a bit *competitive*. Recently, I was cornered by a freelance art critic who—upon learning that I was acquainted with the great Koren—droned on about how Ed's compositions and their captions evince an ideal marriage of exquisite draftsmanship and an ear perfectly pitched for human fatuity, and that virtually any given Koren work renders, with a narrative complexity worthy of Breughel, a richly textured panorama.

I think it would please Ed to hear this, and I would have gladly repeated it to him—except that it has been quite a while since he dropped by. So I offer here: Ed, come back! My door remains open. Your ingratitude is forgiven! And perhaps, if you can find the time, we could bring in a focus group and try to come up with a satisfactory compromise on the whole noses business.

—MARK SINGER

QUALITY TIME

"*Not now, Benjamin—Daddy's having a little quality time with himself.*"

"This song is dedicated to our parents, and is in the form of a plea for more adequate supervision."

"Love you!"

"How were you born? Because your daddy gave some of his pollen to a bee, who gave it to Mommy."

"According to this, everything we've done up to now is right."

"How old is your cabbage?"

"He's just discovered French Baroque organ music."

"Your work holds up quite well, Ben."

"My dear, may I suggest a little old-fashioned biofeedback, some acupuncture, and a dollop of nutrition counseling?"

*"Daddy has to clear his head for a few minutes
before he can deal with 'Babar.'"*

"*I envy your talent—I never had much luck*
with cactus."

"*Have you determined yet whether you will or will not eat your cereal?*"

"Mother of four, meet mother of three."

*"My goodness, it's little Benjie! You've grown
into quite a distinguished man!"*

N and S PET SHOP

$50 REBATE

$25 REBATE

$100 REBATE

KOREN

"*She's not very good at defending herself, but she does*
very well at identifying her feelings."

"Is this the man behind the woman?"

"Ooh! How <u>cute</u>!"

"*Please help us reduce our garbage and improve our energy efficiency and our water quality. Help us to be eco-wise and—above all—to empower others.*"

"*Sometimes he gets so excited he forgets to use his verbs.*"

"*Mom, is this the one about the little engine with high self-esteem?*"

"Henry is into total loyalty."

"My mom says to come in and have a seat. She's on two lines
and has three people on hold."

"*No more carbohydrates until you finish your protein.*"

"*Mark is my partner in quality parenting.*"

"I'd like my daughter to know something about engines."

"Something you should bear in mind, James. Sam has recently come into a lot of money."

"*This is a great place to bring up children.*"

"*Hey, man, to us you're just Bob. Around here,*
we don't do well with last names."

"*Timothy, success is nothing to fear.*"

"*Miranda is in a lot of pain over the attitude of her cat.*"

"My appearance this evening is funded, in part, by the family fortune."

"She's very driven."

*"It sure is great to have you back for
a while at the mother ship."*

"*I'm beginning to think it's salsa that's causing your mood swings.*"

KOREN

"We're just family."

"Mom, can me and Nat go down to the corner store and get some sorbet?"

*"I know I haven't been much of a master to you, but then again
you haven't been much of a pet to me."*

"*Can you believe this is happening to me?*
Her scores are very low in self-esteem."

"That's the famous Josh—a high-impact body harboring a very low-impact mind."

"*Often, it's sullen and withdrawn, and then, suddenly,
it becomes hostile and vengeful.*"

"Do you ever miss New York?"

"You've been a very, _very_ bad sibling."

"That's my mom and dad. They've just returned to traditional family values."

"Grandpa Windsong, tell us another story from the sixties!"

"He's very depressed. There were no messages for him today on the answering machine."

"We've been admiring your fathering techniques."

"*This is my slender volume of poems.*"

"*The fish is on the top shelf of the fridge. The beans are in the blue pot. The salad greens are already washed and in the plastic bag. And if you want to wait, Daddy will make a yummy dessert when he gets home.*"

"*I'm four and change.*"

"How long have you and Charlie been together?"

"*This is an imaginative new concept in the use of leisure time.*"

"Both of you are rotten and hateful—from a kid's perspective."

"*Pay Princess no heed, Ben—she's not used to having men around.*"

"For the last time—Daddy doesn't do sports."

"*Catherine would like to share some holiday thoughts with us on the subject of gender-neutral toys.*"

*"If you promise to be very careful, Mommy will
let you carry the baguettes."*

"Don't worry. He doesn't bite."

"We sing her to sleep with songs about recycling."

"We can't tell yet if it's a malfunction or a dysfunction."

"And after the prime rate declined by half a point, and the Dow rose by thirty-two, guess what happened to Goose and Fox?"

"*You may not recognize Bobby. He's turned into his father.*"

"He loves to be petted."

DIVORCED, VISITATION
EVERY WEEKEND
SINGLE MOM
PEGGY WEBB
JOINT CUSTODY
BLENDED FAMILY
WORKING ON
THE ISSUES
KOREN

"Once upon a time, there was a frozen pizza, and inside the pizza some very bad monsters lived. Their names were refined white flour, reconstituted tomato, and processed cheese. But the worst monster of all was called pepperoni!"

"*I never get what I want.*"

"Maybe you can understand it better this way, Rich. In Act I, Scene 7, Lady Macbeth, who has a heavy foot, is putting the hammer to the firewall. Macbeth is not too comfortable with this, so he is riding the brakes!"

"*Everyone in our family has a commitment to something.*"

"*Looking good! Feeling great! And soon to be famous!*"

"Listen to me, John. Tell them this is our final offer. Let 'em know we'll take an option at twenty-five million over five years—not a penny more, not a minute longer! If they balk, stall them for time and get back to me."

"That's a bird, spelled b-i-r-d."

"*Honestly, Kate—can you picture <u>us</u> in a shopping mall?*"

"*Ezra, I'm not inviting you to my birthday party, because our relationship is no longer satisfying to my needs.*"

*"You've got an irate client on 3, an impatient supplier on 1,
an anxious child on 5, and an angry wife on 2."*

"'Good' is not good enough."

"We still can't decide whether she's more a Hillary or an Allison."

"Pop, you've got to be more supportive of Mom and more willing to share
with her the day-to-day household tasks. Mom, you have to recognize Pop's
needs and be less dependent on him for your identity."

"*That's* fathering."

"Oh—pardon the expletive—<u>damn</u>!"

"AAAAALLLLLL RIIIGHT!"

"His first fax."

"They're museum quality!"

"*Around here his word is law.*"

"*We are looking for the non-yucky apparel.*"

"We have what you young people might call an old-fashioned marriage—we are <u>not</u> best friends."

"How are her scores?"

"Can't you see? He needs both of us!"

"Frankly, your mother and I think you did better work when you were two."

"Do you, Daisy, promise to love, honor, and, in particular, obey Mr. Singer? To beg, sit, stay, heel, and roll over until death do you part?"

"Your father and I want to explain why we've decided to live apart."

"She's family."

"*Do you want to talk about it?*"

FINAL CLEARANCE ENTIRE STOCK OF KANGAROOS

KOREN

"*I'm about to experience the totality of who I am!*"

"*She turned fourteen years old this week, but we think she's ageless.*"

"*I've <u>done</u> my tour of duty on Wall Street.*"

"May I remind you that our prenuptial agreement called for <u>me</u> to take the plants?"

"Nicholas, I want to thank you for sharing."

"We never laugh together anymore."

"*I've just bought five acres of prime oceanfront. Want to help me build on it?*"

"*Tonight, we'll be eating hot dogs with a mustard-ketchup-and-pickle purée, accompanied by peas lightly sprinkled with ketchup. Then fettuccine al dente with a ketchup sauce, followed by applesauce maison with a dollop of you know what!*"

"*Alexa here is my sixty-eight-year-old, and Nat here is my seventy-two-year-old.*"

*"Catherine, we agreed—you would put on your mittens
when your hands got cold."*

"*We have a very special relationship with our barber.*"

"There are some words I will not tolerate in this house—and 'awesome' is one of them."

"*Don't come on too strong, Mark—she's not playing with a full deck.*"

"Ben is in his first year of high school, and
he's questioning all the right things."

"Ah! It's the woodwind family!"

"Charlotte's opinions do not necessarily reflect those of her husband or children."

"*That cat is what's wrong with this country.*"

"*Nicholas, you are to address me as 'Larry,' not 'sir.' Is that clear?*"

"Noah, I'm tired of doing battle with you!"

"*He's a very fussy eater.*"

"*I hate you! You don't understand me and you don't understand my software!*"

"*Sam, neither your father nor I consider your response appropriate.*"

"*Some of us long for the days of the old taboos.*"

"*My dog's name is Kierkegaard, my cat is named Virginia Woolf, I call my car Amadeus, and my boyfriend's name is Freddy.*"

"*Alexandria, you possess a very large talent.*"

"I want you to know I'm angry and hurt."

"Hey, you guys, don't you remember? The big word here is 'compromise.'"

"We're a great team, Sash—you with your small and large motor skills,
me with my spatial awareness and hand-eye coordination."

"We wanted you both to know—we've adopted a humpback whale."

"*In light of the continuing fiscal crisis, Nat, I suggest you reconsider your ambition to be a fireman, a policeman, or a member of the Sanitation Department.*"

"*When the children have all grown up, we hope to move back to the city.*"

"Would the twenty- and thirty-somethings move a little closer to the eighty- and ninety-somethings?"

"*We've decided not to have children.*"

About the Author

ED KOREN is a regular contributing cartoonist for *The New Yorker* and has illustrated sixteen books. He lives in Vermont with his family and their cat.